GHASTLY and GHOSTLY

DEVON

Sally and Chips Barber

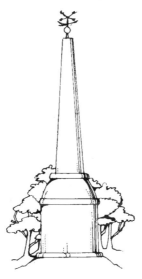

OBELISK PUBLICATIONS

OTHER OBELISK PUBLICATIONS

In this series:

Dark & Dastardly Dartmoor, *Sally & Chips Barber*
Weird & Wonderful Dartmoor, *Sally & Chips Barber*
The Ghosts of Exeter, *Sally & Chips Barber*
The Ghosts of Torbay, *Deryck Seymour*
The Ghosts of Berry Pomeroy Castle, *Deryck Seymour*
The Ghosts of Brixham, *Graham Wyley*
Tales of the Unexplained in Devon, *Judy Chard*
Haunted Happenings in Devon, *Judy Chard*

Also:

Around & About the Haldon Hills, *Chips Barber*
The Lost City of Exeter, *Chips Barber*
Diary of a Dartmoor Walker, *Chips Barber*
Diary of a Devonshire Walker, *Chips Barber*
The Great Little Dartmoor Book, *Chips Barber*
The Great Little Exeter Book, *Chips Barber*
The Great Little Totnes Book, *Chips Barber & Bill Bennett*
The Great Little Plymouth Book, *Chips Barber*
Ten Family Walks on Dartmoor, *Sally & Chips Barber*
Made in Devon, *Chips Barber & David FitzGerald*
Burgh Island & Bigbury Bay, *Chips Barber & Judy Chard*
Tales of the Teign, *Chips Barber & Judy Chard*
Dartmoor in Colour, *Chips Barber*
Exeter in Colour, *Chips Barber*
Torbay in Colour, *Chips Barber*
Plymouth in Colour, *Chips Barber*

All drawings and Cover by Jane Reynolds
Maps by Sally Barber
All photographs by or belonging to Chips Barber
Thanks to WJ Reynolds for his help and suggestions

First published in 1992 by
Obelisk Publications, 2 Church Hill, Pinhoe, Exeter, Devon
Designed by Chips & Sally Barber
Typeset by Sally Barber
Printed in Great Britain by
Sprint Print, Okehampton Place, Exeter

Ghastly and Ghostly Devon

It is estimated that at least one person in every ten will have some sort of ghostly experience at some stage during their life. Therefore, in Devon alone, with a population of about a million people, it is not difficult to work out that around one hundred thousand spooks will make a guest, or rather a ghost, appearance sooner or later. Obviously these will vary greatly in their scope and their scale and this little book takes a look at just some of the strange and bizarre goings on in Devon (although we have stretched a point and put a tentative toe over the border to Somerset for a couple of tales).

It is noticeable that there are certain occupations or professions which appear to create a higher incidence rate of manifestations than others. It would seem that life (or that final cut off point we call death) is amenable to teachers, accountants, solicitors, bankers, civil servants and other white collar workers. When did you last hear of a spectral accountant gliding through a locked door clutching a pile of ledgers?

The few select professions which seem to be at odds in crossing the great divide are, somewhat surprisingly, parsons, priests, abbots, vicars, nuns and monks who crop up more than any other category of person. Possibly this has occurred because they have been close to the action throughout their lives. Or is it perhaps that people such as these, dressed so conspicuously, draw attention to themselves, whereas the 'ghosts' of ordinary people drift quite happily amongst us unnoticed?

Monks must rank among the more passive members of society and indeed their ghosts tend to drift around rather than pop in or out. At Tavistock two monks were seen, by a couple of clergymen, walking in meditative fashion through tunnels beneath Bedford Square. It is believed this labyrinth of subterranean passages once linked parts of the old abbey complex of buildings. Bovey Tracey's monks were creatures of regular habit who ascended a staircase, in one of the town's houses, at the same time every day. These upwardly mobile monks were only heard and not seen, but it is believed they were monks because the staircase had been obtained from Buckfast Abbey and bore the signatures of several monks underneath. Far from being a threatening experience, the children of the house made a point of being around to hear them go by. The phenomenon stopped when there was an

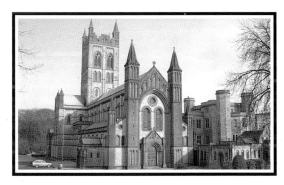

invasion by the media. Perhaps the thought of a feature backed by a soundtrack like 'There are Three Steps to Heaven' was too much for these mild mannered monks!

Buckfast Abbey had its own ghosts in Victorian times. Before the present Abbey was built a group of monks in white or grey made regular appearances. These, like an Abbot from Bradworthy in West Devon, may have been disturbed by the Dissolution — a period in our history when many monasteries, nunneries, abbeys and the like were put out of business. This abbot refused to accept the situation and still haunts Abbot's Lane!

At the village of Abbotskerswell ('Kerswell' means a spring of water), on the outskirts of Newton Abbot (the New Town of the Abbots) is St Augustine's Priory which is now a group of residential flats. However in the 1890s the ghost of a monk appeared, in broad daylight, beside a horse and trap and ran beside it for a considerable distance before fading away. About thirty  years later Mass, being celebrated in the chapel, was interrupted by a shining vision of the Virgin Mary. This was seen by many people.

Hartland Church in north west Devon has an extremely high tower that looks out over fields to one of the most wave battered coastlines in the kingdom. By

contrast its graveyard is a haven which has been visited by the ghosts of monks on more than one occasion. One person's testimony you would probably believe is that of the vicar, Rev Harold Lockyer, who was the vicar of Hartland in 1973. He was adamant about his two sightings. First a monk appeared for the briefest of moments inside the church, then on another occasion a monk appeared moving around amongst the tombstones. When Rev Lockyer approached the monk to greet him, the ghost dissolved into thin air! Perhaps it is just as well that he did, for the unsuspecting vicar may have been subjected to a far worse experience ...

We first stumbled across the story of the Murderous Monk of Lidwell Chapel many years ago when putting together *Around and About the Haldon Hills*. Since then further details have come to light to form a tale which is most likely half truth, half myth. It is a good example of how a minor incident over six hundred years ago can develop into a full blown murder story.

Lidwell Chapel is real enough, despite its ruinous state, and is located on the steep upper eastern slopes of Little Haldon. Its site is well chosen as the brow of this upland tract of moorland protects the site from the vagaries of the weather brought by the prevailing wet and overenthusiastic westerly winds. Just above this location is one of the finest vantage points in Devon, with tremendous views, particularly away across Lyme Bay to the east.

Lidwell was a wayside chapel, dedicated to St Mary, where travellers seeking a place to rest their weary bodies for the night could stay. Despite its high location it had a well called Well of Our Lady or Lady Well (hence Lidwell) in the north east corner of the chancel of the chapel. It was also one of the deepest wells in the area, so deep in fact that a stone plummeting down took many seconds to make a splash.

Communications in 1329 were sadly lacking and depended largely on word of mouth. The Bishop of Exeter (Bishop Grandisson) got to hear that Robert Middlecote, a clerk of Lidwell, had been guilty of defaming the Bishop. To seek confirmation of this he despatched one of his men to go and make enquiries. A trial followed, held in June 1329, the outcome being that Robert Middlecote was found guilty and it is likely that he was labelled as a 'son of perdition' or a 'satellite of Satan'.

Through the hazy mists of time this story became increasingly more gruesome. For now our 'monk' is guilty of some extremely anti-social behaviour, totally unbecoming to his vocation in life. Written accounts vary in detail. A mild version relates how the monk fed and watered his guests before robbing them whilst they were asleep. But in other versions, he lured the travellers into his cell, to hear their confessions, before brutally murdering them and hurling their bodies down the very deep well. This latter version is 'confirmed' by reports that when the well was inspected, it contained many bodies — including several women and children.

A more complete story tells of a sailor taking a land route back to his hometown. Instinct told the sailor that something was not quite right — he was suspicious of the way the monk acted. Still the sailor stayed long enough to share a meagre meal and then excused himself to retire to bed as he had walked many miles that day and was weary. But the sailor was not as tired as he had professed and only pretended to be asleep. The monk waited for what he thought was a suitable period of time, then crept into the room with murder on his mind. Just as he was about to strike, the sailor leapt from his bench-like bed and frantically fought for his life. Fortunately the sailor was both younger and stronger so he overpowered the murderous monk and managed to throw him down his own well — which just goes to show that all's well that ends well!

But this story does not end here. The monk obviously felt cheated as his spirit has haunted the well for many centuries since. It is one of those ghosts which has a limited repertoire, going through the same never ending routine time after time. Climbing from the deep, dank darkness of the well, the monk strives to escape from his watery grave. With great effort he inches his way towards the top of the well. Each time he does this he only just manages to raise his head and shoulders into the daylight, before slipping back down and facing yet another fruitless attempt at escape. However, he is not alone in his hauntings because visual manifestations of murdered women and children have also been seen in and around the ruins; even when not seen, they have been heard screaming or sobbing.

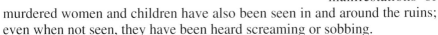

It is a sad, lonely place not far from the traffic which passes across the top of the hill and within easy walking distance of the large car park where couples like to spend an hour or two in romantic pursuits blissfully unaware of the dark and dastardly events which occurred nearby.

For those who have enough courage and curiosity to want to make a visit, this little sketch map should help you to find it. It is well concealed and you will only see it when you are within yards. From the main large car park on Little Haldon, walk on the left hand verge of the main road towards Teignmouth for about 80 yards. You will see a sign indicating a footpath away to your left which follows a rough track. In about another 50 yards you will encounter a

To
Exeter

Car
Park

Little
Haldon

Stile

Stile

remains of
Lidwell Chapel

Golf
Course

B3192

To
Teignmouth

fence and a stile which you should negotiate with your normal nimbleness and panache, making sure that you do not strangle yourself with the strap of your camera hooked solidly on the stile whilst you try marching away from it! (Here speaks the voice of experience!) The track is discernible and leads straight downhill becoming steeper and flintier as it proceeds. Take care not to let gravity get the better of you as a fall on this flint scree would be almost as bad as anything the ghostly monk might have in store for you!

Lower down the hillside, but still on the open common, the track forks. Take the right one and the steepest short section takes you down to a gateway and yet another stile. Now well practised in the art you should gleefully leap over it into the field. Here the soils are better than the commonland you have just crossed. If you follow the fence down on the left side of the field you will find the mad monk's domain and the remains of his chapel awaiting your inspection. Sadly it may seem like an anti-climax as there isn't much of the building's fabric left standing. Provided you have some energy-giving tablets in your pockets, the return journey up the hill shouldn't be too bad. The total trip down and back is less than a mile ... but it might seem longer!

Devon has its share of professional parsons but it must be said that in the past many of them were no better a person than the next man, simply choosing the profession as a soft option, an easy life without too many stresses and strains. Take for example Parson Froude who ended up in the back of beyond at Rackenford. He was a typical country parson who delighted in fox hunting, fishing, riding and drinking. It is hard to work out just what is supposed to have troubled his spirit but he is said to ride a jet black horse at night through this small village.

Another vicar who appears to be unwilling to break free of his mortal coil is the Rev Thomas Kitson of Torquay. In life he was clearly identifiable in a crowd as he was very tall, and as thin as a rake. In fact he was so small boned and thin that he earned the nickname 'Darning Needle'. His afterlife ride is on a white steed which he rides up and down the busy thoroughfare of Shiphay Lane in Torquay.

But the most sinister vicar, who might well have been expected to make a return visit, was Rev Parker of Luffincott.

Now, even people who have a good knowledge of Devon

will probably have never heard of the small hamlet called Luffincott, for if ever there was a quiet backwater this is it. Luffincott is in the Tamar Valley and sits on a hill just a quarter of a mile from the River Tamar, the boundary of Devon and Cornwall.

The pace of life in this parish has always been slow, almost static at times, even by Devonshire standards. The Rev Franke Parker knew this and was more than happy to take on the living, in 1838, which paid him quite well without demanding too much from him. The remoteness was not a problem for the bachelor rector because it enabled him to indulge in his own interests — without the focus of attention that a more largely populated community might give him. In time he was to jealously guard his paradise of peace, privilege and privacy.

The Rev Parker was an eccentric who had many unusual interests, including the occult and Black Magic. In his travels he collected many publications on these matters, taking care to keep them safely under lock and key. He instructed his servants that they were never, under any circumstances, to look at them!

For a Victorian he was, apparently, quite open about his bizarre personality and would pronounce that he had the power to turn himself into a toad or a lion or even a dog. (It was not uncommon for him to be seen sitting in doggy posture barking loudly at the top of his voice.)

When addressing parishioners, he insisted that they should take care to bury him as deep and as securely as was physically possible when he died. This instruction was given with the warning that if they didn't heed it, he would rise again and return. In 1883, after some 45 years as incumbent at Luffincott, the Rev Franke Parker finally went to meet his Maker.

The eleven years following his demise appeared, on the surface, quiet and idyllic. Locals became quite sure that their eccentric priest had gone to rest in peace. During this period there were two successors both, unlike the Rev Parker, married men. But these rectors did not settle, quickly moving on to pastures new, although the job was regarded as an easy one in this lovely rural setting. The Rev Parker had, in his long incumbency, made many improvements to the Rectory, making it a most pleasant abode. The setting was splendid with a footpath running a short distance down to the banks of the Tamar. So was there something about the Rectory which was not quite right?

In 1894 the Rev T.W. Browne appeared on the scene. He hadn't come far, for this promotion brought him from neighbouring Clawton where he had been curate. He had been described as 'a peculiar old chap' although he was not all that old. It was more likely that as a bachelor who loved solitude he had become very set in his ways, and he was more than pleased to remain in lonely exile in this far flung outpost of Devon. He was not a fit man and carried a disability which had left him partly paralysed, so this appointment was a blessing for him — or so he must have thought.

The Rev Browne had little choice but to live alone in Luffincott Rectory because his means were limited. Initially he was happy and lived life without any aggravation but one evening, whilst he was having a meal with his head buried in a book, he felt a presence in the room. On looking up he was horrified to see the ghost of a Rector stood before him.

This must have really put the wind up the Rev Browne. Despite his physical handicap, he got out of the Rectory so fast he left all his possessions behind. Moreover he never set foot back there again, choosing to leave everything, including his books and papers,  behind. He even forbade anyone from getting them on his behalf, seemingly resigned to writing off the Rectory and everything that was in it.

Although Luffincott and surrounding farms are sparsely populated, word of what had happened got around very quickly. Despite enquiries and pressure on the priest, he would not divulge any further details about just what the ghost of Rev Parker had done or said to him to reduce him to such a quivering wreck.

Some locals exhibited great bravado and spent several nights there to see if the Rev Parker would appear to them, whilst others looted the Rectory of its contents. But the Rev Parker didn't appear again and the Rectory fell into a sad and derelict state. Vagabonds and other wayfarers used it as a temporary refuge until, presumably, on one of those occasions a fire was started and the Rectory was totally destroyed — its remoteness assuring it of being well out of reach of any fire engine.

After the haunting the Rev Browne went back to his previous accommodation at Clawton, where he was among friends. He still carried out his duties at St James Church, Luffincott — fortunately the church was a few hundred metres from the Rectory which meant that he didn't have to go too near it. He made sure he always travelled in company and between Sunday services ate his meal in the porch in the sanctuary of the church. However, this arrangement obviously wasn't too satisfactory as he only kept it up for a short while before resigning his living and leaving the district, never to be heard of again.

At the other extreme of Devon, its eastern end, is the small village of Uplyme, situated as close to Dorset as Luffincott is to Cornwall. A nineteenth

century situation here was remarkably similar, with a previous Rector haunting his successor — at the dining table at meal times. This time though the new Rector was made of sterner stuff and, when he could stand no more, he resolved the situation by going and sitting on the ghost! Perhaps if the Luffincott priest had been on an assertiveness course, he could have held his post.

Country parsons of the past often had enough money and enough time to become well and truly eccentric. A South Hams vicar, of substantial means, rode to church in his chariot every week. When he died several farm labourers, who worked the fields around the parish church, swore that they could still hear the distinct sound of his chariot wheels trundling along the lane. So vexed were they by the situation that they employed twelve different parsons, unsuccessfully, to exorcise the ghostly parson.

Then someone suggested that perhaps it would be better if the priest performing the ceremony didn't know the vicar in question. Indeed it was a case of thirteenth time lucky for the ghostly chariot wheels no longer rumble between the high hedged banks of the quiet South Hams lanes.

The distant memory of a former Bishop of Exeter — Edmund Lacy — is kept alive in a pub named after him at Chudleigh, a short distance from his former bishop's palace. It has been suggested that it is he who haunts this pub, although all the sightings indicate it is a monk. The party tricks he plays include stealing silver spoons, turning up the heating and readjusting people's watches.

A most unusual ghostly appearance of assorted clerics is said to have happened at Combe Martin, in North Devon, in the late summer of 1921. This

was witnessed by a visiting lady artist who described a ghostly procession which included a medieval-looking bishop in full regalia, a number of priests, six strong men carrying a large model of a walled city, and ladies, courtiers and peasants — all in fourteenth century costume. Unfortunately nobody else in Combe Martin saw it.

Not too many miles from Combe Martin, but many hundreds of feet higher above sea level, is the location where a cowardly crime was committed. This time the clergy's role was a dynamic determination to seek the truth and bring a murderer to justice.

A lot of people would be content to live in the same location where the Burgess family made their home in the middle of the nineteenth century. Their small, remote cottage, high in a tributary valley of the River Barle, was the sort of place which only the occasional passerby might stumble on by accident. In this retreat an alcoholic miner, William Burgess, and his wife produced three children in what was probably a perfect setting for them to grow up strong and healthy individuals. Whilst Mrs Burgess worked hard and cared for the children everything was fine, but Mrs Burgess became ill, and died in 1857.

William was then landed with the responsibility of the children, a situation he didn't relish so he decided to remove them from the scene. His two older children, Tom and Emma, were dispatched to a farm at North Molton some miles over the hills and away to the south. They were put into service, to be useful to an employer and no longer a drain on their father's liquid assets.

For reasons best known to himself, William took his youngest child, Anna, who was seven years old, with him into lodgings in Simonsbath. It would appear that he resented the half a crown a week it cost him to keep Anna so, one Sunday in June, he announced to his landlady that he was taking his daughter to stay with her grandmother at Porlock Weir.

He duly packed her belongings into a bundle and set off. Poor little Anna did not get to Porlock Weir. William Burgess visited his mother alone and returned to Simonsbath the same day.

Decent folk were suspicious of his actions from the start. The landlady later testified that she saw a small fire behind the pub late that day and was sure that in it she could discern the remnants of some of the little girl's clothing, smouldering amongst the ashes. But because it was 1858, on remote Exmoor, communications were extremely limited and there was no speedy way of discovering whether or not the little girl had been taken to Porlock Weir. Was it not beyond belief that the girl's own father could have murdered her in cold blood and then buried her in a grave on the lonely, wind-swept moor?

A twist of fate almost solved the question quite quickly. A group of William Burgess's drinking pals stumbled over a newly dug grave but, because it was sheep stealing country, they thought that someone had placed a sheep here ready for removal after dark. It made a good story to tell over a glass of ale and they let Burgess into their plans to nip back and recover the carcass for themselves — Burgess was thrown into a panic at how close he was to being discovered. As soon as it grew dark, Burgess was off as fast as his legs could carry him. He dug Anna's body up and carried it a mile to the remains of the Wheal Eliza Iron Mine. This was the perfect place to dispose of a body — several hundred feet deep and flooded with water. He parcelled the body up and dropped it down the deep shaft.

This manoeuvre was not easy as he stumbled about using the darkness of night as a perfect cover. What he did not realise was that someone else was also up to no good, in the same vicinity.

Burgess left the district on the Thursday of the same week and made his way to Lynmouth where he boarded a vessel bound for South Wales. The added barrier of the Bristol Channel between him and those he left behind was psychologically encouraging.

It was following his hurried departure that the local priest, Parson Thornton, came into his own — sweeping into our story like a Victorian version of Columbo. He had a long standing score to settle with Burgess, enough to motivate him to root out this villain and bring him to task. But first he had to confirm whether or not Anna was still alive.

He asked a local forester to go to Porlock Weir and ascertain if the girl was with her grandmother. This was done discreetly and the priest was not surprised to discover she had not been taken there at all. The next logical step was to look for a grave or her body. The empty grave was soon discovered, but this only made the matter more puzzling for Parson Thornton. However he felt there was enough evidence to have Burgess arrested.

The wheels of justice were set in motion; Burgess was located in the Swansea area and brought back to Exmoor. Having been charged with Anna's murder, he was remanded in custody at Dulverton. However, despite regular searches of the moor, the girl's body was not found and Burgess's release, through lack of evidence, looked imminent.

Simonsbath
Car Park
Church
B3223
B3358
River Barle
Wheal Eliza

And then the wheel of fortune turned to favour the Parson in his quest. Obviously the story was on everyone's lips, where could he have hidden her body so successfully that intensive searching could not locate it? One person who heard the gossip had a shrewd idea of just where the body might be — he who had heard suspicious activities on that late and dark June night at Wheal Eliza. Naturally this man faced quite a dilemma as at the same time he too had been perpetrating some misdeed and an admission of his own presence was a confession in itself. Fortunately, there is no 'honour amongst thieves', particularly when the crime relates to a child, so, having wrestled with his conscience, he prepared a statement and gave it to Parson Thornton.

This must have seemed heaven-sent evidence to the Parson and it was enough to persuade the magistrates at Dulverton to hold on to Burgess whilst the mine was pumped out and inspected — quite a bold initiative as they were prepared to pay for the operation themselves if nothing was found!

Through the autumn of 1858 there was steady activity at Wheal Eliza and by November the mine was sufficiently safe for a volunteer to descend to see if Anna's body was down it. A crowd gathered and were able to witness the pitiful sight of Anna's remains being finally brought up.

Amongst the crowd there were several locals present who were not in the slightest doubt that Anna had been down that mine. They claimed that ever since that sad day in June when the little girl had disappeared, a glowing light or flame had been seen hovering over the top of the shaft. They were convinced that this was Anna's spirit of light and were sure that when she was given a proper Christian burial that it would no longer appear.

At the trial of her father, which turned out to be little more than a formality, William Burgess acknowledged that his impending doom was largely attributable to the dogged way in which Parson Thornton had pursued him. He met his end by the hangman's noose at Taunton Gaol on 4 January 1859, just seven months after performing his evil deed.

Poor little Anna now lies at peace in the graveyard at Simonsbath and some say her little light still shines there from time to time.

Simonsbath lies in the heart of some strikingly beautiful countryside, just a few miles beyond the Devon border. There is an excellent walk from this small Exmoor village to Wheal Eliza. There are toilet facilities and picnic area at the car park just below the church. From here you walk down the road and opposite is a path to the remains of Wheal Eliza. This path runs along the hillside, just above the River Barle and is prone to be muddy after rain so it is well worth wearing walking boots or wellies! From Simonsbath it is less than a mile to the old mine workings. An information board just beyond the footbridge, over the river, reveals many details about the mine's former activities including its role as 'Uncle Ben's Gold Mine' in R.D. Blackmore's *Lorna Doone*.

A child's spirit which did not accept its murder in quite such a gentle manner as Anna, haunted a house at Stowford. His apparition ran through the house, time and time again, calling for more rope so that he could avenge his killing. He had been a young child, left an orphan when his wealthy parents died. His wicked uncle cruelly murdered him for the inheritance, but the guilt of his action played on the murderer's mind. He kept re-enacting his immediate action of going down to the nearby river to wash the blood from his hands until in a matter of months he was considered so insane he was committed to an asylum. The ghost of the child is said not to have rested until the uncle died.

Occasionally a haunting will result in the demise of the building like, for example, in the quiet town of Axminster in East Devon where there used to be an inn called The Dolphin. Here the guests were often rudely treated, and one, a travelling Jewish pedlar, was even murdered. He came back to haunt the inn so frequently that custom diminished drastically. It was put on the market but, as there were no takers, it was demolished.

At Drewsteignton, on the eastern borders of Dartmoor, is a cottage where another murder was committed long ago. Every year, at midnight, on the anniversary of the devilish deed, a trickle of blood seeps underneath the front door of the cottage and into the road. This spot is still referred to, locally, as Bloody Corner.

There is another Bloody Corner between Appledore and Northam, quite probably where a Civil War conflict resulted in bloodshed. Young people are supposed to show some respect by removing their boots so as not to disturb the souls or spirits of the dead who perished here, be they Roundhead or Royalist. At the bewitching hour a ghost of a large white horse is said to gallop around at this spot.

At Ottery St Mary there is a particularly fine church which dominates the skyline. It has been nicknamed East Devon Cathedral as it it bears all the architectural attributes associated with such an edifice. Within its north aisle is the statue of Captain Coke. The Cokes were obviously not a very close family as this captain was a victim of fratricide, having been murdered by his brother. His statue is believed to come alive at midnight and rush around the church.

One of the major problems for murderers down the years has been how to get rid of the body or bodies. These days people tend to joke that our concrete motorway bridges play host to many victims of gang land crime, but concealing a victim in so solid an unconventional tomb is not a new idea — variations on the theme have gone on for years. But worse, the victims in the past were often not dead first!

At Berry Pomeroy Castle, near Totnes, poor Lady Margaret was imprisoned and starved to death. Her fate was decreed when she fell in love with the same

man as her jealous sister. She still stalks the tower, now named after her, where she was entombed. For this story and numerous more about Devon's most haunted castle, read Deryck Seymour's book *The Ghosts of Berry Pomeroy Castle*.

At Holcombe Rogus, a village which has won numerous Best Kept Village titles, there was an unsavoury discovery which reflects the social attitudes of past centuries when the stigma attached to illegitimate births made it border on the realms of a cardinal crime, even though it was a common occurrence. The treatment meted out to those unfortunate girls who got pregnant out of wedlock was often nothing short of scandalous. However, a seventeenth century Squire, John Bluett, who was about to marry into a rich and titled family, must have committed a far greater sin in anyone's eyes when he discovered that his extra curricular activities had put a local maiden into the 'family way'. He locked up the mother and child in a tower of his large house and allowed them to starve to death before concealing their bodies. Two centuries later, the owners of the house discerned the sounds of faint crying, like that of a baby. When they later embarked on some building work, the remains of a woman and small child were discovered and given a Christian burial. The child's voice has not been heard since.

As a nation, the majority of us are accustomed to living in fairly modest dwellings, the number of rooms usually corresponding to the size of our families. To most of us it is a purely romantic idea that one day, when effecting some repairs, we might stumble accidentally across some secret, hidden room. However in larger houses this has happened on a number of occasions, and sometimes the finds have been gruesome.

The most notable Devonshire discovery was at Chambercombe near Ilfracombe, in North Devon, in 1865. The room which was discovered contained a four poster bed with its curtains drawn. Imagine the horror the poor Victorian must have felt as these curtains were drawn back to reveal the cobweb-covered skeleton of a lady lying on the bed. Weird noises emanate from this room and Chambercombe Manor is no stranger to the sound of nocturnal footsteps in and around many parts of the property. The girl's bones have been reburied in a local churchyard although nobody knows who she was.

Although one would never condone a crime of passion, it is at least possible to understand why, in the heat of the moment, an ordinary person can be guilty of an outburst of brutality which is totally alien to their personality. At Weare Gifford (pronounced Jifford) in the valley of the River Torridge in North Devon, a moment of madness led William Dillon to murder his beloved in a fit of pique. The dark deed was committed in the garden at Hazel Cottage, in late May 1887. Overcome with remorse and guilt, Dillon slit his own throat but made a terrible hash of his suicide. It took an agonising fifteen days for him to finally die and in his pain he begged forgiveness for his crime. It is the ghost of the murdered girl which haunts Hazel Cottage and not the troubled spirit of William Dillon.

'Forches' is a name which appears on the map and also in house names in many places throughout Devon. There is one on the hillside of the valley of the Arch Brook, a tributary of the River Teign, near Stoke-in-teignhead. There is another on the outskirts of Newton Abbot and one at Rewe near Exeter. In fact they are liberally splattered around Devon but most people are unaware that this is another name for a gallows, a place where people paid the price for their illegal indiscretions.

There are also hills in Devon, a favoured location for making 'examples' out of felons, which derive their names from their former gruesome function. The Little Hangman Hill, high above Combe Martin, is well named. It is believed that a sheep thief unwittingly executed himself whilst in the process of committing his crime. The rope that he had attached to the sheep somehow became wrapped around his neck. As the poor creature (that is the sheep) struggled in its bid for survival, the thief was strangled!

An interesting use of place names exists on this dramatic heather covered hill. The portion of land to the immediate west is called 'evidence' whilst that which lies to the south is referred to as 'witness'. Case proved m'lud.

A tale is told of a similar incident on the outskirts of Torquay at a point where the road runs past a place where a 'market' is held every Monday in the warmer months. This point is called 'Gallows Gate' and from this high point there are also tremendous views towards southern and eastern Dartmoor and across Tor Bay and South Devon. Alas yet another sheep thief would not have appreciated the panoramic view as he, too, managed to garrote himself. The cord tied around the bag holding the sheep again found its way to the neck as the man slipped climbing over the Gallows Gate.

By topping themselves both men managed to cut out both the middle man (the judge) and also cheat the executioner.

As many of our other publications have covered the amazing story of John Lee, we will briefly only state that at Torquay this man was accused of murdering his employer. At Exeter he was found guilty but, despite having the most experienced hangman in the business for his chop, all three attempts to execute him failed miserably. For further details see the *Lost City of Exeter*.

An amazing aspect of John Lee's story is that he had a dream that he would not die, and told of it as a firm and correct prediction. Having been proved right, at least he stopped there and didn't turn himself into a 'prophet' like Joanna Southcott.

Every so often a 'chosen one' is born and that privileged person takes it on board to be a centre of much attention and speculation. They appear at random and range from former Coventry City goalkeepers through to poor Devonshire farm girls. As Joanna Southcott never played in goal for the Sky Blues, it can be assumed she falls into the latter category.

Born in 1750 in the geographical remoteness of the tiny village of Gittisham

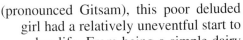

(pronounced Gitsam), this poor deluded girl had a relatively uneventful start to her life. From being a simple dairy maid she moved on to become a humble domestic servant. Her nomadic nature took her on to work in various small shops in and around the Exeter district. She was an honest and devout girl who became greatly involved with the Wesleyans, a band of worshippers particularly strong in the South West.

At one of her religious meetings she met a 'visionary'; she was influenced by his prophecies and soon got in on the act herself. She started modestly enough with a weather forecast here and there. Having enjoyed a degree of success she changed to prophecies in the political climate. Her predictions were somewhat hit and miss. The hits were acclaimed — the misses were either forgotten or glossed over. She developed a technique of writing down her predictions on paper and then sealing them. These were put away until they came true. If the prophesies weren't fulfilled, the sealed papers weren't consulted. Thus her success rate and her fame grew accordingly.

By the age of 42 she was acclaimed as a prophetess. To generate her success she paid a printer to produce her predictions. He not only did the printing but also spent a considerable time correcting her poor spelling, punctuation and grammar!

In London she confronted bishops and church leaders with her predictions and acquired herself a vast following. However, at the age of 64 she surpassed herself. She told the world that she was pregnant and that she was going to be the mother of the second Messiah. A great house was lavishly prepared for this event. But Joanna was sadly awry in her prediction. She was not pregnant. Her swollen abdomen was a medical condition called dropsy. Instead of giving birth, she died. The gathered crowds were stunned by the news and, almost inevitably, there were those who refused to accept the truth.

As a legacy, she left a box of prophecies, a cure-all prescription for all humanity, in a locked box which was to be only opened in the presence of 24 bishops. The box remains closed as those conditions have not been met and the world remains in a state of turmoil — all it needs is a ceremony to put things right!

To our knowledge Joanna Southcott has not returned to haunt Gittisham or

Sidmouth, where there used to be an enthusiastic Southcottian Society confident of her return.

From Joanna's prophesies and dreams we move on to a large house on the opposite site of the county when a man's dreams lead to a murderer's comeuppance ...

Some six miles to the west of the great high rolling moorlands of Northern Dartmoor lies Hayne Manor, reputed to be one of the most haunted houses in Devon. This large house, close to Stowford, is sited in the valley of the River Thrushel. However the house can boast an even longer history for much of the stone used to build it was taken from Haine Castle higher up the hill. The castle was owned by the same family but it had become too draughty, was in a state of disrepair, and was regarded as being 'too old fashioned' — all those centuries ago!

Duly built, Hayne Manor has had more than it fair share of famous visitors and resident dignitaries. Just one example was John Harris, who was Master of the Household of both George II and III. Needless to say a house which was well staffed and which entertained a vast number of well known characters over several centuries has to have its skeletons in the cupboard, and its subsequent ghosts.

About the middle of the eighteenth century John Harris took his second wife (his first having died) Ann, daughter of Lord Conway. As mistress of the house she organised the staff so that everything ran like clockwork. Her particular favourite was a young page who went about his servant's duties in a cheerful and obliging manner. So it was a shock to Anne when he went missing along with some of the valuable household silver.

Immediately messengers were dispatched to Exeter and Plymouth to alert pawnbrokers to keep a look out for the stolen silver. The butler appeared duly concerned at the loss of the silver and made efforts, beyond the normal call of duty, in an attempt to track down the stolen goods. However the weeks, months and years rolled by and there was no sign of the silver or the servant boy. The incident mellowed in the memories of the family and eventually it was more or less forgotten.

Two Tiverton farmers visited Hayne Manor for the Court Leet proceedings, an annual court of record held by the steward of any hundred, lordship or manor. In this instance they had journeyed more than forty miles on horseback to pay their annual rents so it was natural for them to stay the night at Hayne Manor. The farmers retired to bed after they had socialised for a while.

One of them soon settled into a deep sleep for it had been a long day. However he had a vivid nightmare which disturbed him so much that he broke out into a sweat. The next day he was troubled because he recognised the butler as being a central character in his dream, but he said nothing and dismissed it as a change of environment from his normal secluded rural existence.

The day of the Court Leet's transactions occupied the farmers for many hours and the business didn't conclude until late afternoon. As it was too late to start home, the men stayed on for another night. However the farmer experienced exactly the same vivid dream as the previous night. In it, as clear as crystal, he witnessed a scene where the young page boy from many years earlier, caught the butler and the housekeeper stealing the silver. On being discovered, the butler killed the page. The farmer's dream took him to a yew tree in the grounds where he saw how the butler dug a grave and buried the page together with some of the silver. At this point, in a terrible state, the farmer awoke from his dream.

John Harris calmed the farmer down and sent the butler off on an errand. Whilst he was away the farmers and John Harris went to the tree and soon discovered the body and the silver. On the butler's return, he was confronted with the evidence and he confessed to the crime.

At Launceston he was tried and found guilty and became the last man to be executed there.

Another gruesome tale from Hayne involved the huntsman who went out to quieten the hounds when they were disturbed, wearing only a somewhat immodest nightshirt. Members of the household were aghast the next morning when all they found were the huntsman's bones as the hounds had completely gobbled him up!

In the garden of Hayne are a number of monuments which include one to the page boy and another to the huntsman. Another ghost of Hayne Manor includes a Roundhead soldier who is said to walk around the house in a happy state, with his head tucked tidily away under his arm. At the time of the Civil War the house owners were staunch Royalists and were instrumental in providing much support for Charles I. The Roundhead soldier's execution had been ordered by an occupant of the house and he was happy to be seen in ghostly form walking around the house because he was fortelling the imminent demise of the head of the household!

A black dog, the spectral type, was seen many years ago and a little old lady ghost, who nobody has recognised, has pottered about in ghostly innocence on occasions. To cap it all a nearby wood is believed to be cursed as two murders were committed there when the land was a corn field.

Thrushelton is a tiny village quite close by and is sited just to the north of the A30 road. Although it appears to have no ghosts, its church bears a relic of a tragic incident which occurred in August 1788. Valentine Jory was out in the fields working as an agricultural labourer. It is probable that he was spreading dung on the fields when the Grim Reaper paid a sudden visit. Whether or not it was an accident or the influence of some potent cider, we shall never know, but Valentine slipped from his cart and fell beneath the wheels of the vehicle. The weight of the dung cart was sufficient to crush him. Jory's gory story upset his employer, Arthur Tremayne, so much that he kept, as a morbid memento, the wheel of misfortune. A descendant of the employer, Captain Gervaise Babington MC, found it amongst family possessions and decided

to present it to the Parish of Thurshelton in 1948. It was given the honour of being mounted in the entrance porch of the church along with the accompanying written details relating to its grim past.

It would seem as if more pubs are haunted than graveyards and there are legions of landlords ready, willing and able to tell of their horrible hauntings. After all a pub ghost in a tourist area can be a positive boon and far from being put off, trippers actually like a scary tale to accompany their ale.

We have had many such stories told to us but when they are accompanied by some sort of historical basis of truth it adds to the overall interest.

Buckland Brewer is a hilltop village about five miles to the south west of Bideford. Although today it is off the proverbial beaten track, it is a sizable village that boasts a thirteenth century inn. In Arthur Mee's *Devon* (1952) he states that "The inn is ancient beyond record, and has been used as a court house; in the beams of the very low ceiling are rings to which the wrists of the prisoners were fastened." Those rings were used on numerous occasions whilst justice was meted out to those brought to trial. The likelihood of anyone either getting off lightly, or getting off at all, was lessened because one of the judges to preside there was none other than George Jeffreys, a Scottish born judge who was notorious for his brutality. Ultimately he acquired the label 'the Hanging Judge' —quite apt as it was 'curtains' for the hundreds of people paraded before him, often for crimes which were, by our standards, petty, but which resulted in the most severe of sentences.

At The Coach and Horses the judge would do his work and stay the night, no doubt sleeping soundly. Those who were sentenced to death were taken upstairs to be executed. A narrow flight of stairs led up to the hanging room where the victims were strapped to the ceiling. A trap door in the floor permitted them to drop to their doom down into the court room below. Needless to say in such an environment there must have been a lot of men and women wrongfully convicted and killed, so ghosts in this pub are far from being unexpected and it has been known for them to occasionally walk around upstairs when it is known there is nobody up there. The pub's most disturbed or noisiest period was the 1950s when shadowy figures were often spotted upstairs and a cacophony of sound emanated from various parts of the pub, particularly from above the trap door.

Fortunately Judge Jeffreys did not enjoy a long life himself and died in the Tower of London at the age of 41 in 1689. However, Judge Jeffreys cannot be held responsible for all the pub's ghosts for many of them hark back to a time before he was even a twinkle in his father's eye. This area of Devon was a battle interface between the Parliamentarian forces and the Royalists during the English Civil War. It is believed that a lot of hacking went on between these two sides in the neighbourhood and some awful injuries were inflicted.

One lady customer saw two cavaliers in the corner of the inn where the trap door used to be. As she approached to greet them, they disappeared before her very eyes. At Christmas 1978 another of the shadowy figures appeared and remained long enough to be identified as a Roundhead. Just before the person who saw it could scream, he disappeared. It certainly seems to be the case here that the ghosts do not like sudden gestures or reactions from the living. This raises the question to provoke lengthy discussion: "Do ghosts still appear when people are not around to see them?"

Incidentally Judge Jeffreys is supposed to haunt a number of places which include the White Hart Hotel in South Street, Exeter and the castle/dungeons at Lydford on the edge of Dartmoor

— where he is also supposedly to assume the form of a ghostly black pig. This is strange because in real life he never visited Lydford!

Sometimes a gruesome tale is told not to attract people, but to keep them away ... in *Dark and Dastardly Dartmoor* we wrote of a most odd tribe of red headed cattle rustlers who lived in caves in the ground on the steep sides of Lydford Gorge. Although their behaviour was regarded as peculiar and irksome to the local populous, it palls into insignificance compared to a family who lived in a cave at Clovelly several centuries ago, long before the days of donkeys and audio visual shows.

John Grieff, or Gregg, who came from the Exeter area, and his wife produced eight sons and six daughters. They went duly forth and multiplied, often incestuously, with alarming regularity, to create a further fourteen grandsons and eighteen granddaughters. This family of tribal proportions certainly required some feeding, particularly over the long, harsh winter months. But, despite living in a cave by the seaside for maybe 25 years, they never ever left home to go shopping for provisions. They survived by abducting any traveller or passerby, robbing and then killing them, before disposing of the bodies. The gruesome rumour was that their larder was stashed with 'long pig' or, to the uninitiated, human flesh! An equally horrific notion is that, before this was discovered, many an innocent person had hanged upon suspicion of committing the crimes!

Obviously to keep up this lifestyle for quarter of a century, a vast number of people would have had to have been murdered, some estimates being as high as 1,000 victims. When it was discovered that the North Devon population was being decimated, attention turned to the Grieffs. Capturing them would not have been a task to take on lightly so a posse of around 400 men, with bloodhounds, undertook this unsavoury chore. The contents of the cave they found was not a sight for the faint-hearted — piles of limbs, and bodies hanged up in rows like dried beef, some in pickle.

The Grieffs were taken to Plymouth and executed without a trial as there was sufficient evidence that they were creatures beneath human dignity. Indeed, they all died without any sign of remorse or repentance, cursing and swearing right to the end. Their ashes were allowed to blow away in the wind.

If you think this story is maybe just a trifle too much to swallow, perhaps we should admit that not many people believe it to be true, it is far more likely to have been a ploy put about to keep prying eyes away from the caves where smuggled goods were safely stowed away!

The county of Devon may be a quiet backwater to urban folk in their over sized cities, but that does not make it a stranger to violence, even in the tight-knit community at Peter Tavy, a small village tucked snugly beneath the hills of western Dartmoor. A century ago everyone knew everybody and most people knew their neighbours' business, but such familiarity in this cosy community led to murder ...

William Williams of Peter Tavy was smitten with young Emma Doidge. His feelings for her bordered on the obsessional — which was a great shame for these emotions were not reciprocated. So it is understandable how poor William felt with every smile or look that was offered by this seventeen-year-old girl to anyone of the opposite sex. He was particularly jealous of another William who lived in the village, of whom Emma was fond. Twenty-two-year-old William Rowe was another Peter Tavy man and, like the other two involved in this emotional triangle, was from a long established family.

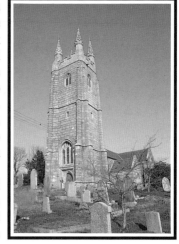

Tired of having his romantic notes and messages to Emma ignored, William Williams went to nearby Tavistock on 8 November 1892 and purchased a revolver at an ironmonger's shop. Williams secreted the revolver beneath his coat and proceeded to church at Peter Tavy. Almost everyone went to church in those days so Williams knew Emma would be there together with his rival for her affections, William Rowe.

Williams' emotions were on a knife edge and in church managed to become engaged in an argument with Emma's brother. No doubt this was a talking point for Emma, her sister, her brother and William Rowe as they headed for home. Unbeknown to them, Williams, wracked with jealousy, had anticipated their movements and had rushed out to lay in ambush for the approaching party. As they reached a certain spot in the lane he jumped out and challenged them, brandishing his revolver.

His first actions were certainly premeditated. He shot and killed William Rowe. He then briefly argued with Emma before shooting her dead too. All hell was then let loose in this quiet moorland lane whilst Williams added to the mayhem by trying to commit suicide, 'trying' being the operative word!

His first attempt merely wounded himself in the head. He staggered to his feet and pulled the trigger again. This time his aim was more sure, but still he only managed to shoot out most of one eye. Screaming, blood everywhere, Williams rushed from the scene, crossed some fields, and jumped into the River Tavy to drown himself. Judging by his run of bad luck that day, it will be no surprise that this too failed! Finally, unable to kill himself, he gave up.

His case did not come up until the following March when Williams pleaded 'not guilty' to murder on the grounds that at the time he was insane. The judge, however, would not accept the plea and justice took its course when Williams was executed on 28 March 1893 for his 'crime of passion'.

Our next story takes us back to Exmoor, which straddles the Devon/Somerset border. Here a young girl met a terrible end and it has never been proved whether she was murdered by human hand, or whether the moor itself drew on a sinister mantle and lured her to a lonely death.

Gwendoline Mollie Phillips was known as Mollie to her many friends in the Exford area of Exmoor where she lived. Not yet eighteen, she was a strong healthy girl who had lived in the area all her short life and knew it like the 'back of her hand'.

The summer of 1929 had been a very dry one and the weather on that September 8th was hot and sunny. Mollie decided that a visit to her aunt at Cutcombe would make a pleasant Sunday afternoon excursion. Being a good country girl who enjoyed the fresh air it didn't matter that the local bus wasn't running — she had thought she might catch it but was just as happy to walk on such a pleasant day.

She had bade farewell to the housekeeper at Rocks Farm just after lunch, promising to be back before dark but, as darkness descended on Exmoor that night, concern began to grow when she hadn't returned. That concern turned to panic when it was discovered that she had never, in fact, made it to her auntie's house!

The next day a massive search was organised over an extensive area of Exmoor moorland, with no success. The search was stepped up and an army of volunteers combed a 50 square mile area of Exmoor. A local pond was emptied but to no avail. The search parties included many people who had great expertise and knowledge of their environment as many of them either rode the moors for pleasure or hunted with the local hounds. Despite extensive searches nothing emerged and the girl's total disappearance was a complete mystery to the local populace.

And so the mystery continued for nearly a year and a half until, one March day, two men, out burning down some grassland, noticed something strange protruding out of a nearby bog. On close inspection they found, to their horror, that it was the largely decomposed skeleton of a young woman. It was beside a spring of water and embedded against it was a large stone weighing about 30 pounds.

The authorities were called in and this grim discovery was identified as poor Mollie.

The task of extricating the girl's body from the bog was no easy matter. The police officers found themselves on very 'shaky ground'. They had to dig deep trenches to drain the water away and then fill them in with grass tufts.

An autopsy revealed no broken bones or any other obvious sign of injury or assault.

The inquest was held at Minehead and there was no attention paid to choosing a jury of people familiar with the nature of the environment involved in this incident. After considering all the evidence it was decided that Mollie had died of shock from exposure and that she may well have drowned in that bog. The jury agreed on a verdict of misadventure but also added an opinion that Mollie could have been hurrying away in fright from somebody — which was inconsistent as that would have been manslaughter, if not murder! But what other explanation could there be, for the bog in which she was found was miles from her intended route that day and there was no logical reason for her to have been there at all.

The Rev Arthur Courtenay Jenoure had made up his mind as to the cause of Mollie's death.

He conducted her funeral service at Cutcombe Parish Church and uttered these words, amongst many more, on the matter.

"I am quite certain that ninety percent of the population of this district believe Mollie Phillips to have been foully murdered ... we are asked to believe the feeble story ... that this powerful young woman, who knew the moor well, ran into a bog, which, in all probability, at that time of year, did not exist, and that she quietly lay there and died without a struggle ... the verdict of the jury would have been a disgrace to a jury of twelve year old schoolboys!"

Following statements like this the police were stirred into action and the boggy area where Mollie was found was drained and dug over and they recovered Mollie's spectacles, a buckle from her belt and a hair slide. Whilst this was going on a horserider spotted their activities and rode up to see what was going on. However, less than twenty yards from the scene, his horse suddenly sunk in the mire up to its stomach and only a skilled bit of horsemanship helped it escape. This incident was a notch up for those who favoured the accidental death verdict because a major point of contention was — were Exmoor bogs able to be killers? This incident seemed to answer 'yes', but this happened in the spring of 1931 whereas Mollie's death was at the end of a long dry summer. Not many locals believed it was possible.

And so the case remains open for debate. One aspect that does not seem to have been satisfactorily cleared up is that the Rev Jenoure received a lot of mail from people either congratulating him on his campaign, or telling him to leave well alone. But one letter was from a man in Wales who claimed to have seen a 'vision' of a man and a girl arguing. The man had strangled the girl and then dragged her body up a hill before dumping it into a swamp. If you add to this a statement made to the police by a Timberscombe woman (that a man she knew to have been 'fond of Mollie' claimed that he knew where Mollie Phillips was — shortly before he departed the area for ever) you might conclude that perhaps Mollie never really set off to visit her auntie that day. Perhaps she had a rendezvous with that young man ...

At Hartland Tor on Dartmoor there is a commemorative stone placed in memory of William Donaghy who died close by, although various authorities have suggested that it is not sited in the exact spot.

William Donaghy, aged 33, lived with his two sisters, quite happily, so it appeared, in his home town of Liverpool. His workdays were spent at nearby Warrington where he was employed as a science teacher. However, on the 21 November 1913 he carried out his teaching duties in the morning but failed to make it back for the afternoon session. Needless to say his superiors were none too happy with his unexplained disappearance.

Unlike Mollie Phillips' disappearance, his was apparently preplanned. A few days earlier, William had withdrawn £50 from his bank, a substantial amount in 1913, which he had given to his brother with the express wish that it be used to settle any matters needing attention. His brother had not been unduly surprised as he knew that William had been suffering from stress, for which he was receiving medical treatment. When he disappeared his family assumed he had gone away for a few days to think and come to terms with life. But, just like Mollie, the days turned into weeks and the weeks into months and there was no sign of him at all.

The many people who knew and liked this quiet and religiously devout man would never have guessed that Dartmoor, in distant Devon, would be his chosen destination. On 21 February 1914, exactly three months to the day after he had disappeared, his body was discovered on the side of Hartland Tor, on the East Dart River, just about half a mile upstream from the famous beauty spot of Postbridge. It looked as though William had succumbed to the extremes of the weather which had been some of the worst that Dartmoor could conjure up. What was strange was the total lack of equipment or protection he had with him, and it was also most peculiar to find his body lying on top of a groundsheet and not wrapped up in it.

It was never discovered what he did or where he went in the missing months. It seems that he had assumed the name of Jones so as not to be identified. There was nothing to suggest foul play and there was no suicide note, unless one he wrote had been blown away in the wind. On the dead man's person was £20 in gold and silver coins and a cloakroom ticket for an Exeter railway station. From this it was possible to work out Donaghy's movement's, at least for his last few days. In a locker at the Exeter station there were various personal effects which included a revolver and plenty of cartridges. Was he planning suicide but, unable to take those last fatal steps himself, chose instead to walk from Exeter across Dartmoor and down to Plymouth, letting the severe Dartmoor weather take its toll before finally laying down to die a more peaceful death? We shall never know precisely what his intentions were or his state of mind was at the time.

After his inquest, which was held in a crude tin shack at Princetown, the *Western Morning News* ran a sub heading which described the facilities as 'An apology for a Mortuary' because some of those present had almost died from exposure too!

Death is nature's way of saying slow down. It also provides a steady flow of 'clients' for the undertakers, but even funeral directors have been known to have to deal with their share of 'awkward customers'!

At Ilsington on the edge of Dartmoor, about 1800, a lady died at her house which was on the lower slopes of this hilly parish. When the time came for her funeral the four horses which had been harnessed to the hearse were all in a highly agitated state, foaming at the mouth, and refused to climb the hill to the graveyard. The priest was summoned and the spirit of the lady is said to have been laid, but her home, for some time afterwards, continued to be the source of many inexplicable noises.

By virtue of its size, the wilderness of Dartmoor has always posed problems

for those whose dearly departed needed a burial service. Most of the wilder parts of Dartmoor fall within Lydford parish, the largest in England. This meant those who died on the edges had a long haul in order to be taken to the parish church which lies on the north west edge of Dartmoor. A route was forged across the remotest tracts of moorland and was called 'The Lich Way', meaning the way of the dead. Along this route the ghosts of monks and funeral processions have been seen on various occasions. However this type of apparition is one of the more common ones, perhaps a reflection that the funeral is a lot more painful to those participating than the death itself.

Another obvious trigger mechanism for creating ghosts is the non-compliance of the deceased's burial wishes. This is almost sure to result in the return of a disorientated spirit. At Bickington a lady was not despatched to the plot which she had booked. She made her point that she was not at all happy with the situation by appearing each day, walking down the village street in her plaid shawl. By so doing she maintained a routine which she had carried out in her latter days.

Sir Walter Gifford also occasionally goes on a ghostly walkabout. His soul is restless because, for some unknown reason, he is not buried with his wife. He glides from his manor house and along the road to the churchyard in Weare Gifford, passes through the Lich Gate and proceeds to the church door. Here the polite knight knocks on the door, which spookily opens without human help, and he enters the church.

Whilst the mourners were attending Squire Usticke's funeral, he was still at home terrifying his housekeeper by entering the room and sitting in his favourite chair!

The Rev Jack Radford was the rector of Lapford for thirty six years and in that time people reckon he expounded enough energy for double that time span! His life was steeped in controversy as he was charged with murdering a curate. Despite being found 'not guilty', he knew that the powers that be would not be happy to consent to his wishes of being buried in the chancel of his church. In anticipation of this he warned that his ghost would return to haunt the church. When he died he was laid to rest in the graveyard but it is hard to keep an active person still, even after death. The cross on his grave would not stay in place until ultimately it had to be cemented into position to stop it falling over. His ghost has been seen in the church, in the graveyard and also down in the village of Lapford.

Death for Madam Margaret Gould of Lewtrenchard in West Devon was not the end but simply the beginning of a series of adventures which she embarked upon as soon as she was free of the shackles of her earthly body. At the precise point of her death, in 1795, all the windows, doors and shutters of the extremely

large and spacious house flew open. Less than hour later one of her servants saw her roaming in the garden. As a freed spirit she visited her favourite 'haunts' and was seen out on Galford Down at other spots which she frequented as a young and vibrant lady. Indeed almost some forty years after her death, a carpenter had been called into the church to do some work when he chanced upon her coffin. Curiously compelled to peep in, he obviously wished he hadn't when Margaret promptly sat up, opened her eyes and began to chase the carpenter out of the church! Had a stop watch been placed on him there is no doubt his mile long sprint back to his home would have beaten all records! Despite his great haste Margaret kept up with the carpenter long enough for his wife to witness the ghost. Ever since she has been heard or seen in this vicinity at regular intervals. Her favoured spot for appearing is down by the banks or